Tricks and Treats

Elizabeth Guerra

BookLeaf Publishing

Presentation by *BookLeaf Publishing*

Web: www.bookleafpub.com

E-mail: info@bookleafpub.com

ISBN: 9789357747776

First edition 2023

For my daughter Lilith. Keep being uniquely and authentically you.

ACKNOWLEDGEMENT

To my family and friends, thank you for being my constant source of inspiration.

PREFACE

A collection of poems with a dash of darkness and delight.

All Hallows Eve

On the night of Hallows eve.
When the moon is full and bright.
I long to be awoken.
By the creatures of the night.
To be whisked away like magic
As they flutter through the air.
While the cauldrons slowly bubble, and cackles
are heard everywhere.
To be dancing with the goblins by the pumpkins'
glowing light.
And see dead souls giving loved ones one last
eery loving fright.
So come stroll with me at midnight, on the night
of Hallows Eve, for the night is full of magic
and spooky wonders to be seen.

Skin Walker

There's a creature in the darkness. He skulks about at night. Looking for lost souls to steal and indulge in their demise. He might look like your friend; he might look like a foe. Or pretend to be a lone wandering crow, but the moment he has you within his grasp, take a deep breath, for it will be your last.

Hooded Figures

5

Hooded figures above the grounds.
Witches, goblins, ghosts and clowns.
Some are scary, some are shy, flying around in
the October sky.
Enjoy the wonder and delight in the magic of
Halloween night.

Headless Horseman

Searching for his missing head, is the rider of the undead. He rides once a year on All Hallows' Eve, searching for a head to cleave. This ancient creature as legend tells, won't stop until he drags you to hell. To try and get vengeance for his missing head, soon you and your loved ones will be dead. So tread lightly when you hear him ride, or you might be the next to die.

Bleeding Heart

Somewhere down the road of life,
I tripped and fell and found a knife,
Which I used to carve my name into your
bleeding heart.
I laughed, you screamed, Oh, what a dream to
see you bleeding love.
What's wrong my dear? Isn't this fun?
Don't try to run now I'm not done!
This punishment is but a gift.
From the one you used to love.
So Instead of lies, I'll take your eyes,
Instead of tears, I'll give you fears,
HOLD STILL my love, don't make a mess!
You're getting blood all on my dress!
HUSH now my dear, do you not hear? The
carriage of your death draws near.
Rest now my dear, don't be afraid. You'll soon
be sleeping in your grave.

Trick - Or -Treat

They come once a year on the night of Hallows Eve. Some asking for Tricks, some asking for Treats. Enjoying the breeze of the cool October air, hoping with their costumes they're able to scare. Enjoying the night eating goodies galore, as merrily they carry on door to door. So come and be a part of the spooky delight, and enjoy the wonders of Halloween night.

Spooky Luly

Spooky Luly, Spooky Luly, made of Porcelain and clay.
Spooky Luly, Spooky Luly wants to follow you and play.
She'll bat her eyes and turn her head and terrorize you for a while. She'll steal your soul and drive you insane as she giggles and she smiles.
She'll watch your every move whether you're near or far and if you try to get rid of her, She'll always know where you are. She's here to stay and here to play, this haunted little dolly. So do your best to keep her impressed. Try not to get lost in folly.

Dark Prince

He's full of darkness and obsessed with pain. Some say he's even a tad insane. His devilish smile and seductive touch will have you feeling an electric rush. Porcelain skin and deep red eyes, it won't be long before your demise. He'll catch your gaze and caress your lips, before he gives you his immortal kiss. The last thing you'll feel is his icy breath, as slowly you succumb to your death. So hurry now and rush home lad, be weary of dear old Prince Vlad.

Deadly Companion

17

He picks his victims one by one.
Some are old and some are young.
But do not worry, don't you distress. When the
time comes for you to take your rest. He'll
quickly show up by your side when the moment
of your death arrives. Dark and hooded holding
a scythe. He'll slowly guide you as you fade into
the night. He'll walk with you while you roam,
through the darkness for your eternal home. Will
it be heaven or will it be hell?
Only time will be able to tell. Life is not fair or
so they say. But we're all doomed to share the
same fate.

Lone Wolf

There's a howling in the distance, a sudden rumbling through the trees, red eyes brightly peering at the life he had to leave. Once a handsome prince, doomed to forever hide, for no one around is safe when the moon is full at night.

Little Vampire

In a crooked old house, down an empty dark road, here lived a little vampire stuck in bed with a cold. Unable to fly, bat his wings, or play games. He took a sip of blood and in his coffin remained, for if he wanted to fly and give the humans a fright, the little dark prince had to rest for the night.

Lechuza

Welcome my children, and hear my tale, of a creature most foul don't miss any details. Legend has it they say that on Halloween Night, this creature emerges from the depths and takes flight. Disguised as an owl she'll fly round and round, looking for her next victim to scoop off the ground. It's easy to spot if she's circling by, you might hear her whistle, cackle or cry. Don't be fooled by her tricks, for she won't hesitate. To drag you to hell where you'll soon meet your fate.

The Monster Inside

There's a monster inside me
At times he wants out…
But I try my hardest to quiet him down.
The world sees my smile, my innocent face.
But at times he whispers. " let me have just a
taste"
He says, "Oh come on, what's the harm? Let us
have some FUN!
Let us watch them squirm, as they try to run.
Let us watch them, BLEED and their shouts
drown out.
Oh come on my dear, let me out! Let me out!!"
Perhaps there will come a time when I'll let him
win..
and bring about.. every kind of sin...
For now he'll remain in a dormant state.
Dreaming of what hell to bring when he finally
wakes..

Wicked Witch

27

With a snap of her fingers and a flick of her
wrist.
The witches' spell will be hard to resist.
She'll take the lives of both young and old,
To restore the youth that she used to behold.
Then she'll once again take to the skies, to lure
in her next victims and bring about their demise.

SACRED
TO THE
MEMORY

Zombie

On this Hallowed night, while the pumpkins
gleam, and the wind flows freely between the
trees. A creature will emerge from beyond the
grave wrapped in linen and hungry for brains.
He'll wander near and far to search for his meal;
the brains of naughty children are usually ideal.
So do your best to behave or on Halloween
night, this creature might try and sneak in a bite.

Who are you?

I'm the monster that's hiding underneath your
bed,
I'm dark thoughts that are creeping around in
your head,
I'm the shadow flying across the moon,
I'm the sudden sound of impending doom.
I'm the one you wish for and the one you hate.
I'm the last thing you'll see when you meet your
fate.
I'm the echo resounding when nobody is home.
I'm the shiver down your spine when you're
scared and alone.
You can hope, you can pray, but I'll always be
near.
Slowly driving you insane as you disappear.

Pumpkin Jane

Pumpkin Jane, Pumpkin Jane.
The little witch who lived on Sugary Lane.
Instead of flying across the moon,
She marched to the beat of her own tune.
She wasn't scary like the witches of old.
And instead of eating children, she'd eat pie à la
mode.
She didn't have an evil laugh, no bubbling
cauldron, no trusty black cat.
She always knew she was a little bizarre, but she
told herself " Hey, all the best people are. "

Bats In The Attic

There're bats in the attic, I hear them at night. They're planning on giving the children a fright. To make the kids' night on Halloween, be more exciting than it's ever been. They plan on flying round and round, lifting some of them up off the ground. Making funny dances as their red eyes glow, hoping that children will enjoy the show. They haven't agreed on what to do just yet, but I'm sure it'll be a night that we'll never forget.

Little Alice

Little Alice cast a spell that did not end up very well. She tried to make some Dragon Stew, and ended with some slimy goo. It spread completely down the hall, into the attic and up the wall. It went into the neighbor's fence, before you knew it, it got immense. It swallowed cities, lamps, and cars. Who knew making stew would be so hard. Perhaps little Alice will think it through, before she makes another brew.

Trapped

Trapped in the realm of the living,
The spirits of the ones long dead.
Confused and constantly dreaming,
Of finally resting their head.
So they float around in the darkness,
Hoping to come into sight.
To find the one that will lead them and kindly
show them the light.

Forever Halloween

41

They say it comes but once a year,
But I say it's always here.
When you carve pumpkins to scare the dead,
And undead creatures are running ahead.
When vampires are looking for a bite,
Then quickly flee into the night.
When black cats screech as they walk by,
And the witches cackle is heard nearby.
When the lone wolf lets out a howl,
And ancient beasts begin to growl.
The best night of the year is here,
And in my heart forever dear.